Alfred Görgens

Herbs for Cooking

Cookery editor Sonia Allison
Series editor Wendy Hobson

foulsham

Foreword

Fresh herbs, almost more than any other single ingredient, add sophistication to the taste of food and give it an incomparable flavour. Crispy roasts with sage, rosemary or thyme, fresh herb soups with chervil and sorrel, attractive egg dishes with Italian herbs, piquant desserts and herb snacks are just a few examples of how the combinations work to produce dishes of gourmet quality.

As you go through the book, you may find it surprising to see how otherwise simple recipes can be transformed into memorable meals just by adding a few fresh herbs. And the main advantage to their use in cooking is comparatively simple. Many herbs included are ones you can grow yourself and you will find some advice on this in the following pages. Additionally, at the end of the book, there are instructions on how to make herb vinegar and oil, herb butter, basil mustard and how to conjure up many other things such as bouquet garni and herbs de provence.

Contents

Herbs through the Centuries	5
From the Orient to the Kitchen at Home	6
Kitchen Herbs	8
Tips on Growing Herbs Yourself	10
Harvesting and Drying	12
Notes on the Recipes	13
Soups, Starters and Sauces	15
Main Courses	23
Desserts, Biscuits and Extras	35
Index of Recipes	48

Herbs through the Centuries

Fresh herbs do not only provide interesting flavours but they are also healthy. What the ancient Greeks wrote about, modern science has confirmed. The recipes in this book demonstrate that herbs can be profitably used in sickness and in health and in the creation of haute cuisine recipes for every occasion.

From the Orient to the Kitchen at Home

Whether it is herbs for seasoning, as healing remedies for sicknesses, as herb cushions for warding off evil spirits and plagues or as scented lotions with which to bathe and pamper the body, herbs have served mankind kindly through the centuries.

Originally, many herbs came from the Orient and were nursed and tended in the gardens of Western monasteries until they became acclimatised to our cooler weather. Originally the leaves, flowers and roots of herbs were used for healing purposes and as long ago as 2500 BC, the Chinese Emperor Shen Nung described in a comprehensive book the beneficial effects of herbs he had tried out for himself, whereas the earliest herb book in the West did not appear until 2100 years later, written by the Greek Diocles from Carystos. About 300 BC, the first Herb Association was founded. It was a coming together of those knowledgeable about herbs, who called themselves Rhizotomen (root cutters) and their activities were bound up with cult worship of the earth.

This was the birth of herb magic which reached its peak in the fifteenth and sixteenth centuries and which was steeped in questionable accounts of miracles, associated with obscure rituals which took place when the seeds were sown, the herbs harvested and subsequently used for whatever purpose was deemed appropriate.

Astrologers also made use of herbs. They allocated plants to particular birth signs and thus decided which plant was suitable for which person. For Leos, for instance, lovage, saffron, rosemary and camomile were said to be supportive, whereas Aries benefited healthwise from marjoram, garlic, horseradish, mustard and parsley. The most well known astrological herb book is that of the seventeenth century English herbalist and astrologer Nicholas Culpepper whose work has been continually republished to this day and won innumerable followers.

We, today, may grumble about government expenditure on causes to which some of us do not necessarily subscribe but, in relative terms, it is a mere drop in the ocean compared with the vast sums of money taken from state budgets through past centuries to purchase vastly expensive herbs and spices from afar. In the hedonistic days of the Roman Empire, when greed was the order of the day, pepper consumption became incalculable and, from the year AD 176, all spice

The miniatures on these two pages are from the fourteenth century and were taken from the Housebook of Cerruti.

traders passing through Alexandria had to pay a pepper tax. Despite this, traders made a fortune from herbs, cinnamon, cloves, pepper, ginger, cardamom and mace and even the founder of the Muslim faith, Mohammed, was a well heeled spice trader before his religious call.

As with all trading, a bitter fight soon broke out over monopolies and profits. Up to a point, countries where spices came from were kept secret, or one simply kept quiet – as did the Egyptians – about the convenient sea route from Egypt to India in order not to endanger the so-called 'incense route' that led through their own country. As well as this they spread terrible rumours about the 'tremendous dangers' involved in buying in the lands of origin in an attempt to prevent competition from trips to China, India or Africa.

Despite all this, herbs did arrive on the kitchen table. The first professional cookery book author, Marcus Caelius Apicius, who lived in Rome around 150 BC and has left us a ten volume work on the art of cooking, devoted the first volume to herbs, spices and general cooking rules. We learn, for example, that oysters were served with a sauce of pepper, parsley, dried mint, caraway, honey, vinegar and fish brine. Contemporary food books dwell long and hard on the advantages of using fresh herbs, producing sauces not unlike the one Apicius created. We have come a long way since the days of parsley sauce and with the back-up of supermarkets and ethnic food shops, there is a worldwide choice of herbs available, either fresh or dried.

Given that you want to and have some spare time, most herbs can be grown outside in sheltered spots, inside on kitchen window sills, in hanging baskets or on balconies.

Kitchen Herbs

Basil
Fresh basil leaves have an intense flavour and strong seasoning powers. They are suitable for south European dishes, especially those from Italy. The dried herb is milder than fresh.

Savoury
Savoury tastes a little like mint but the leaves are less pungent. It goes well with beans and some vegetable soups and aids the digestion of fatty meats such as pork, lamb, duck and goose.

Borage
Borage leaves remind one a little of the taste of cucumbers and are therefore quite good in salads. Borage is also very good with peas, beans and cabbage dishes. As well as the leaves, the clusters of blue flowers can also be eaten or candied. It is the traditional herb to add to Pimm's No. 1.

Tarragon
Tarragon is a subtle herb much used in French cooking and seasoning mixtures. The leaves are used for seasoning steaks, omelettes, mushrooms and fried fish. Preserved in vinegar, the sprigs contribute a fine flavour and the vinegar is especially fragrant in salad dressings.

Chervil
Chervil is a tender seasoning herb that is best used fresh. The somewhat sweet-tasting leaves, slightly resembling parsley, are particularly suitable for poultry and fish dishes as well as mushrooms, white sauces, grills and soups.

Lovage
Lovage tastes faintly of yeast and, in contrast to many other herbs, keeps most of its seasoning power when dried. This herb is particularly suitable for soups, sauces, casseroles, hot pots and mixed vegetable soups. As lovage has a strong and distinct flavour, it should be used sparingly.

Marjoram
Marjoram has become one of the most well loved herbs in the kitchen. It has a pleasant, aromatic flavour and is well-suited to poultry, vol-au-vent, egg dishes, lamb, soups and Italian-style sauces. It should be used cautiously because it leaves a pungent after-taste.

Oregano
Oregano is another herb widely used in southern Europe, Mexico and the USA and is a natural choice for pizzas and other Italian dishes. Sometimes called 'wild marjoram', it is quite strong in flavour and should be treated with an element of caution.

Rosemary
Rosemary has a strong and distinctive taste and is particularly suitable for game dishes. Used sparingly, it is equally pleasing with poultry, eggs and mushroom dishes. A sprig of rosemary placed in oil makes an aromatic seasoning.

Sage
Fresh sage is strong and pungent and best used for duck, turkey, game, pork and veal. Home-made sausages can be seasoned successfully with sage. Sage leaves fried in batter are a delicacy.

Sorrel
Sorrel can be grown at home or simply gathered in meadows. The typically sour taste of the fresh leaves produces not only a tasty soup, but also tangy sauces for fish and wild duck. Spinach leaves make a possible substitute, provided they are young and tender.

Thyme
Thyme, along with marjoram, is another well loved herb and can be used fresh or dried with fish and egg dishes. Lemon thyme is suitable for desserts, especially vanilla sauce and puddings as well as fruit salads.

Tips on Growing Herbs Yourself

Plant pots, window boxes and garden tubs are very good containers in which to grow herbs, or you can grow them in the garden itself. When buying seeds you should make sure that they are fresh and have come from a trusted and reliable source. There is a distinction to be made between annual, biennial and perennial herbs. Annual herbs must be sown or planted each spring (and some each autumn). They produce leaves, flowers and fruit (seeds) all within twelve months and then die. Borage is a typical example of an annual.

Biennial herbs develop flowers and fruit in the second year after sowing, after which the plants slowly die. Very often, though, the leaves can still be harvested well into the second winter. A typical biennial herb is parsley.

In the case of perennial herbs, the part of the plant above ground will die off in autumn or winter, but the roots remain intact and send out new shoots the following spring. This process can be repeated for several years. Perennial herbs, such as lemon balm, can be propagated quite simply with cuttings.

Growing in a pot
Most herbs can be grown quite easily in a plant pot. Pre-requisites are a light position, facing east or west which should also be free of draughts and excessive strong sunlight. It is not a good idea to place the plant pot above a radiator. Generally pots of 10 cm/4 inches across are suitable. They should be made of clay or stone with a drainage hole as good drainage is essential when growing herbs. Ordinary garden soil can be used, better still potting compost, though take advice from your local gardening centre. Seeds are sown in spring or in autumn (see also tables on page 12).

Seeds should be planted about 2.5 cm/1 in deep in the soil. The soil

should not be too damp or too dry and dry earth should be dampened before seeds are sown. Especially easy to grow are the young plants available now in most supermarkets. These are usually supplied in plastic pots and should be re-potted in clay pots. This can – as with seeds – be carried out in spring or in autumn.

On the Balcony
Anyone with a balcony can place the plant pots of herbs outside throughout the summer or sow directly into boxes. However, herbs do not do well on balconies facing south with permanent sunshine, or on shaded balconies where the heat can build up. Also unsuitable are balconies that suffer from environmental pollution, such as those near a busy main road.

In the Garden
You can start the herbs off in a plant pot and then plant them out in the garden or even sow the seeds directly into earth in the garden. Generally herbs feel at home in a gently sunny, dry position (but read the instructions on the seed packet). The soil should be lightly dug over and be fine and crumbly before sowing and it is a good idea to turn the soil over in the previous autumn. The seeds should be sown about 2.5 cm/1 in deep (or according to the instructions on the packet). Those seeds requiring light in order to germinate are just pressed lightly into the soil. Artificial fertiliser should not be used, neither should fresh manure; the herbs will lose their flavour as a result. Best to use is compost or dry, rotted manure.

During the period of germination the herbs should be watered regularly, but not too generously. Later on – given that it is not too dry – they can be left to nature.

Name of herb	Plant type	Sow plant	Position
Aniseed	annual	mid-spring, sow	sunny
Basil	annual	spring, sow	protected from wind
Bay leaf	perennial	late spring, plant	sunny
Borage	annual	spring, sow	half-shade
Camomile	perennial	spring, sow	sunny
Caraway	biennial	spring/autumn, sow	sunny
Chervil	annual	spring, sow	half-shade
Chives	perennial	mid-spring, sow	half-shade
Coriander	annual	late spring, sow	sunny
Dill	annual	spring, sow	sunny
Fennel	perennial	late spring, sow	half-shade
Lavender	perennial	spring, plant	sunny
Lovage	perennial	spring, sow	half-shade
Marjoram	annual, as the plant is not frost-hardy	spring, sow	sunny
Mint	perennial	spring, plant	damp
Parsley	biennial	spring, sow	sunny
Rosemary	perennial, but sometimes dies in winter here	mid-spring, sow	sunny
Sage	perennial	spring, sow	sunny
Savoury	annual	spring, sow	sunny
Sorrel	perennial	spring, sow	half-shade
Tarragon	perennial	late spring, sow	sunny
Thyme	perennial	late spring	sunny

Harvesting and Drying

Some herbs – such as parsley, chives and sage – can be harvested all the year round. Other biennials and perennials are best harvested in spring, and annuals in autumn. In all cases one should wait until the plant is fairly mature before picking off any leaves and use the older and larger ones first. Perennials should be left to rest from the autumn.

Practically all herbs can be used fresh when harvested. If you want to store them it is best to cut stems at the base with scissors or a sharp knife just before flowering. The basic rule is that the more carefully one handles the plant, the more the aromatic oils will be preserved. Cracked or torn leaves reduce the seasoning value greatly. Harvested herbs should be dried right away and as quickly and carefully as possible. A good place is next to the central heating boiler, a warming oven in an Aga cooker, or a well-aired cupboard with a slatted floor. The herbs should also be kept in the dark. The best temperature is about 30°C/86°F. It will depend on the plant which method is used.

To dry large leaves such as basil or sage, the leave should be laid singly on a tray, wire mesh or a wooden frame across which some muslin has been stretched. Leave the

herbs to dry and turn them over daily. Herbs with small leaves such as dill or tarragon should be wrapped in a piece of paper still on the stalks and hung upside down. Herbs from which the seeds are used, such as aniseed or coriander, should be gathered into small sheaves and threshed after drying in a box or on a tray with a high rim. The drying will take between two and seven days.

As soon as the plants rustle or fall from the stems and no longer bend but break, they are dry. Single leaves of herbs dried on the stalks should first be plucked off and then rubbed in the same way. After rubbing, they can be kept in opaque, air-tight jars, wooden pots or containers. If you have only clear glass jars available, line the inside of the glass first with aluminium foil to prevent deterioration through light. All containers should be labelled and dated.

Herbs that are to be used for special purposes, such as bouquet garni, should not be rubbed. The best thing to do here is to dry the leaves on their stalks. This also applies to herbs used for flavouring oil or vinegar.

Some herbs, such as parsley, lose much of their seasoning value if dried and stored. Others are not affected at all by storage.

Herbs can also be deep-frozen but care must be taken not to crush the leaves or aroma will be impaired. The best thing to do is to put the leaves or small bundles of herbs in rigid plastic containers with well-fitting lids.

Notes on the Recipes

1 Follow one set of measurements only, do not mix metric and Imperial.
2 Eggs are size 2.
3 Wash fresh produce before preparation.
4 Spoon measurements are level.
5 Adjust seasoning and strongly-flavoured ingredients, such as onions and garlic, to suit your own taste.
6 If you substitute dried for fresh herbs, use only half the amount specified.
7 Kcals refer to one portion of the recipe and are approximate.
8 Preparation times include both preparation and cooking and are approximate.

Soups, Starters and Sauces

With fresh herbs, these simple dishes whet the appetite for the main course or give a final touch of verve. Lift your cooking by using delicate aromatic herbs and spoil yourself and your guests.

American Herb Soup, page 16

Tarragon Soup, page 16

Tarragon Soup

Serves 4 to 6
Preparation time: 40 mins plus soaking
735 kcal/3070 kJ

150–200 g/*5–7 oz* dried green peas
1 l/1¾ *pts*/4½ *cups* vegetable stock
30 ml/*2 tbsp* chopped fresh tarragon
30 ml/*2 tbsp* crème fraîche or single cream
salt and freshly ground black pepper

---

1 Soak the dried peas overnight in water.
2 Drain off the water and cook the peas, covered, in the vegetable stock over a low heat for 30 to 40 minutes until soft. About 15 minutes before the peas are cooked, stir in the tarragon.
3 Rub the peas through a sieve or purée in a food processor or blender. Fold in the crème fraîche or single cream and season with salt and pepper. Reheat, stirring from time to time until soup just comes to the boil.

Photograph page 14

Gourmet Tip
The soup can be improved by adding a knob of butter and a pinch of sugar just before serving.

American Herb Soup

Serves 4
Preparation time: 20 mins
210 kcal/890 kJ

---
50 g/*2 oz* lettuce, chopped
50 g/*2 oz* fresh spinach, chopped
1 small onion, finely chopped
a few sprigs tarragon, finely chopped
a few sprigs rosemary, finely chopped
a few sprigs chervil, finely chopped
750 ml/1¼ *pts*/3 *cups* vegetable or meat stock
2 egg yolks
150 ml/¼ *pt*/⅔ *cup* cream or crème fraîche
salt and freshly ground black pepper
¼ bunch chives, finely chopped

---

1 Simmer the lettuce, spinach, onion and herbs in the stock for about 10 minutes.
2 Rub the soup through a sieve then return to the saucepan. Mix the egg yolks with the cream or crème fraîche, add to the soup and cook, stirring, until thickened. Do not allow to boil. Season with salt and pepper then sprinkle each serving with chives.

Photograph page 14

Herb Mushrooms

Serves 4
Preparation time: 30 mins
410 kcal/1720 kJ

---
450 g/*1 lb cup mushrooms*
30 g/*1¼ oz butter*
10 ml/*2 tsp* chopped fresh parsley
10 ml/*2 tsp* chopped fresh oregano
10 ml/*2 tsp* chopped fresh coriander or dill
1 clove garlic, crushed
salt and freshly ground black pepper
2 to 4 tsp/*each 5 ml fresh breadcrumbs*
butter or oil

---

1 Wipe the mushrooms clean with a damp cloth. Twist out the stalks. Trim away the tops then chop remainder of stalks finely. Fry lightly in butter. Add the herbs and the garlic clove. Season to taste.
2 Remove from heat and add sufficient breadcrumbs to make a medium-stiff stuffing.
3 Grease a casserole dish with oil, fill the mushroom heads with the stuffing mixture and place in the dish as shown in the picture. Put 2 flakes of butter on each or sprinkle with a little oil. Bake in a preheated oven at 180°C/350°F/gas mark 4 for 10 to 15 minutes.

Photograph opposite

French Sandwich

Serves 1
Preparation time: 10 mins
275 kcal/1150 kJ

a piece of baguette, about 15 cm/6 in long
15 ml/**2 tbsp** olive oil
5 anchovy fillets
1 small tomato, sliced
1 small onion, sliced into rings
1 sprig basil, freshly chopped
1 sprig chervil, finely chopped
1 sprig parsley, finely chopped

1 Cut the bread along the length and sprinkle with oil. Lay the anchovy fillets on the bottom half then arrange the tomato slices and onion rings on top. Sprinkle with herbs and cover with the second piece of bread.
2 Wrap the sandwich tightly in aluminium foil and leave to stand for 10 minutes for the flavours to amalgamate.

Photograph (bottom)

> **Gourmet Tip**
> If liked, very thin slices of garlic and radishes can be added to the sandwich with the anchovies and vegetables.

Herb Salad

Serves 4
Preparation time: 20 mins
620 kcal/2590 kJ

A selection of mixed leaves to include:

young dandelion leaves (optional)

endive (curly type if available)

chervil

radicchio

5 ml/**1 tsp** *prepared mustard*

10 ml/**2 tsp** *herb vinegar*

sugar

salt and freshly ground black pepper

a few fresh basil leaves, or other herbs according to taste, finely chopped

1 clove garlic, crushed

45 ml/**3 tbsp** *salad oil*

1 Wash and drain the salad leaves. Arrange in individual salad dishes or in one large bowl.
2 Whisk together the mustard and vinegar. Add sugar, salt and pepper to taste. Stir in the herbs and the garlic. Finally add the oil a little at a time, beating the dressing continually. Pour over the salad just before serving.

Photograph (top)

Sorrel Sauce

Serves 4
Preparation time: 20 mins
830 kcal/3480 kJ

25 g/*1 oz* sorrel leaves, finely chopped
200 g/*7 oz* curd cheese
45 ml/*3 tbsp* whipping cream
lemon juice
salt and white pepper

1 Mix the sorrel with the other ingredients and season to taste. The sauce should have a relatively thick consistency. Serve with fish or veal.

Photograph opposite (top)

Health Tip
Sorrel has the effect of stimulating the appetite and purifying the blood.

Barbecue Sauce

Serves 4
Preparation time: 30 mins
975 kcal/4080 kJ

2 medium-sized onions, chopped
45 ml/*3 tbsp* salad oil
2–3 cloves, garlic, crushed
200 g/*7 oz* puréed tomatoes
40 ml/*2½ tbsp* mild vinegar
100 ml/$3\frac{1}{2}$ fl oz/$6\frac{1}{2}$ tbsp white wine
10 ml/*2 tsp* dried thyme, crushed
10 ml/*2 tsp* dried basil, crushed
1 bay leaf
30 ml/*2 tbsp* brown sugar or honey
5 ml/**1 tsp** prepared mustard
salt and freshly ground black pepper
tabasco sauce
Worcestershire sauce

1 Fry the onions lightly in hot oil. Add the garlic, puréed tomatoes and vinegar. Cook for a few minutes over a medium heat.
2 Mix in the wine then add all the other ingredients, one after another. Simmer uncovered, for 15 minutes, stirring occasionally. The sauce can be served cold or warm with grills.

Photograph opposite (centre)

Pesto Sauce

Serves 4 to 6
Preparation time: 20 mins
540 kcal/2260 kJ

25 g/*1 oz* fresh basil leaves, chopped
20 g/*1 oz* pine kernels, ground
4–5 cloves garlic, crushed
50 g/*2 oz* sheeps' cheese
50 g/*2 oz* cream cheese
30 ml/*2 tbsp* olive oil
salt and white pepper
a pinch of sugar

1 Put the basil leaves and pine kernels into a mortar. Add the garlic, sheeps' cheese and the cream cheese and, using the pestle, stir until the ingredients are well combined.
2 Add the olive oil a drop at a time and stir continually until the mixture looks thick and paste-like. Season with salt, pepper and a little sugar. The sauce can be served with pasta, fish, grilled meat and in minestrone soup.

Photograph opposite (bottom)

Main Courses

Herbs do much to enhance the flavour, and sometimes the appearance, of main dishes and make a most attractive garnish.

Lamb Cutlets with Thyme, page 24

Lamb Cutlets with Thyme

Serves 4
Preparation time: 25 mins
1665 kcal/6970 kJ

6 medium-sized lamb cutlets
15 ml/1 tbsp salad oil
20 ml/1½ tbsp chopped fresh thyme
salt and freshly ground black pepper
juice of 1 lemon

1 Press the lamb cutlets flat with the palm of the hand and make a small vertical cut at the outer edge. This prevents the inner surfaces of the cutlet from bulging out during frying.
2 Brush oil on both sides of the cutlets and season with thyme, salt and pepper then sprinkle with lemon juice.
3 Grill under a brisk heat for about 5 minutes, turning once. Alternatively, fry in a non-stick pan with heat fairly high, also turning once.

Photograph page 22

Gourmet Tip
Cutlets prepared in this way can also be barbecued. Serve with a fresh mixed salad and wedges of French bread.

Herb Roast Pork

Serves 4
Preparation time: 1½ hrs
2740 kcal/11470 kJ

30 ml/2 tbsp chopped fresh sage
salt and white pepper
a pinch of ground cloves
a pinch of paprika
a pinch of ground ginger
15 ml/1 tbsp olive oil
1.25 kg/3 lb piece of pork for roasting
1–2 sprigs of sage
3–4 cloves garlic, coarsely chopped
strips of lemon rind from ½ lemon
300 ml/½ pt/1¼ cups medium dry white wine

1 Mix the sage with the next 5 ingredients. Work in the oil then rub the spice mixture over the meat. Other herbs and spices can be used as desired but sage should dominate. Cover and leave in a cool place, for 2 to 3 hours.
2 Transfer the meat to a casserole and arrange the sage, garlic and lemon rind on top. Pour on the wine and roast in a preheated oven at 220°C/425°F/gas mark 7 for about 1½ hours. Every quarter of an hour, baste the roast with the cooking juices. Turn the sage sprig each time and brush it over the meat.

Photograph opposite (top)

Veal Cutlet with Mixed Herbs

Serves 4
Preparation time: 35 mins
935 kcal/3915 kJ

100 g/4 oz mushrooms, sliced
25 g/1 oz/2 tbsp butter
1 small onion, chopped
100 g/4 oz sorrel
2 veal cutlets
salt and white pepper
10 ml/2 tsp chopped fresh parsley
10 ml/2 tsp chopped fresh chervil
45 ml/3 tbsp crème fraîche
50 g/2 oz Gruyère cheese, grated

1 Sauté the mushrooms in one-third of the butter, stirring occasionally. Transfer to a plate. Add the onion with one-third more butter. Cut the sorrel into fine strips and add. Simmer for a few minutes, then remove and place with the mushrooms in a casserole dish.
2 Brown the cutlets on both sides with butter. Season and arrange on top of the sorrel and mushroom mixture. Pour over the cooking juices then sprinkle with the herbs. Spread with crème fraîche then sprinkle with grated cheese. Bake for about 10 minutes in a preheated oven at 200°C/400°F/gas mark 6.

Photograph opposite, (bottom)

Honey Chicken with Tarragon

Serves 4
Preparation time: 50 mins
1300 kcal/5440 kJ

1 chicken
1 onion, finely chopped
25 ml/1½ **tbsp** chopped fresh tarragon
60 g/2½ **oz** butter or margarine
15 ml/1 **tbsp** honey
salt and freshly ground black pepper
90 ml/6 **tbsp** double cream

1 Wash the chicken, then fill with onion and tarragon, reserving about one-third of the tarragon. Put half the butter inside the chicken.
2 Transfer to a greased casserole dish, drizzle with honey then season with salt and pepper. Top with flakes of the remaining butter. Cover the dish with kitchen foil and roast in a preheated oven at 160°C/325°F/gas mark 3 for 30 minutes, basting the chicken with the cooking juices from time to time. If necessary, pour on a little water to prevent dryness.
3 Remove the foil then sprinkle the remaining tarragon over the chicken. Increase the heat to 190°C/375°F/gas mark 5 and continue to roast until the chicken is golden brown, basting periodically with cooking juices.
4 Remove from the casserole and keep warm. Pour the cooking juices into saucepan, and add the cream, stirring continually. Boil gently until the sauce looks creamy.

> **Gourmet Tip**
> Rosemary can replace tarragon if preferred as it goes well with poultry. As a tea, rosemary has soothing effect on an infected mouth.

Chicken with Tarragon in Cream Sauce

Serves 4
Preparation time: 2 hrs
2345 kcal/9820 kJ

1.25 kg/3 lb chicken cut into portions
25 g/1 oz/2 tbsp butter or margarine
150 ml/¼ pt/⅔ cup chicken stock
salt and freshly ground black pepper
10 ml/2 tsp Madeira
1 small bay leaf
3–4 shallots
1 carrot
30 ml/2 tbsp crème fraîche
2 cloves garlic, crushed
45 ml/3 tbsp dry white wine
1 egg yolk
30 ml/2 tbsp chopped fresh tarragon
15 ml/1 tbsp chopped fresh coriander

1 Place the chicken in a large frying pan, add the butter or margarine and cook gently for 20 minutes, gradually adding the stock.
2 Season the chicken pieces with salt and pepper. Pour in the Madeira then add the bay leaf, shallots and carrot. Cover and simmer gently for 1 hour.
3 Arrange the chicken on a serving plate and keep warm. Remove the carrot and bay leaf from the juices. Stir in the crème fraîche and garlic. Mix in the wine, egg yolk and herbs. Reheat briefly without boiling, then pour over the chicken.

Photograph opposite (top)

Chicken Livers with Sage

Serves 4
Preparation time: 30 mins
1025 kcal/4290 kJ

675 g/1½ lb chicken livers
50 g/2 oz butter or margarine
4 shallots, finely chopped
2 apples, peeled and sliced
15 ml/1 tbsp chopped fresh sage
15 ml/1 tbsp sherry or brandy
salt and white pepper

1 Cut the livers into pieces. Heat half the butter or margarine and lightly fry the shallots.
2 Add the apple and sage and fry gently for 5 to 7 minutes, keeping the heat low. Remove and put to one side.
3 Heat the remaining butter or margarine in the frying pan, add the livers and fry on both sides for about 3 minutes, turning once. Add the shallot and apple mixture with the sherry or brandy, season with salt and pepper and bring up to the boil, stirring. Simmer gently for 2 minutes.

Photograph opposite (top right)

Italian-Style Meat Nuggets

Serves 4
Preparation time: 25 mins
1245 kcal/5205 kJ

3 slices wholemeal bread
675 g/1½ lb minced meat (Beef, pork or lamb)
1 onion, finely chopped
30 ml/2 tbsp chopped fresh parsley
30 ml/2 tbsp chopped fresh basil
3 cloves garlic, finely chopped
salt and freshly ground black pepper
90 ml/6 tbsp olive oil

1 Soften the slices of bread in water then remove and press dry. Mix well with minced meat, onion, herbs, garlic, salt and pepper. Shape into smallish meat balls.
2 Heat the oil in a drying pan and add the meat balls. Fry until crispy brown on all sides, turning frequently. After the initial browning, reduce the heat and cook for about 10 minutes.

Photograph opposite (bottom)

Variation
You can also fill the meat balls with cubes of cheese or change the taste by using different herbs.

Rustic Fish Pot

Serves 4
Preparation time: 1½ hrs
3320 kcal/13485 kJ

1.5 kg/3¼ lb different fish and shellfish (cod, hake, halibut, prawns, shrimps, mussels, etc)

a few sprigs fresh mixed herbs

a few peppercorns

8 strands saffron

150 ml/¼ **pt**/⅔ cup olive oil

2–3 onions, finely chopped

2 sticks celery, finely chopped

3–4 cloves garlic, finely chopped

4 to 5 tomatoes, skinned and diced

2.5 ml/½ **tsp** chopped fresh thyme

20 ml/**4 tsp** chopped fresh fennel leaves

1 bay leaf

salt and freshly ground black pepper

wholemeal toast or white bread

1 Fillet the fish and prepare the shellfish. If you ask your fishmonger to clean the fish, keep the trimmings. Make a stock using the heads, bones (and shells where appropriate) with finely chopped mixed herbs, a few peppercorns, saffron and about 450 ml/¾ pt/2 cups of water. Rub the stock through a fine sieve.

2 Heat the oil in a large saucepan, add the onions, celery and garlic and fry gently for 7 minutes. Add the tomato, herbs and spices.

3 First add the fish with the firmest meat, such as halibut. Pour in the fish stock then add enough water to cover the fish. Bring to the boil and leave to cook for a few minutes.

4 Add the fish with soft meat, such as prawns, and leave the mixture to simmer, uncovered, for about 10 minutes. The fish should not be allowed to cook for too long or it will disintegrate. The mussels and prawns should be cooked in a little wine or stock separately and then they should be added to the cooked fish.

5 Put a slice of bread into four deep soup bowls, scoop the fish soup on top and eat while still very hot.

> **Gourmet Tip**
> The soup will have a more distinctive flavour if finely cut orange peel from ½ orange is fried with onions and celery.

Herb Potato Pancakes

Serves 4
Preparation time: 30 mins
810 kcal/3405 kJ

8–10 medium-sized potatoes

30 ml/*2 tbsp* chopped fresh herbs (chives, parsley, chervil, thyme, rosemary, basil, etc.)

4 pinches ground mace or nutmeg

salt and freshly ground black pepper

75 ml/*5 tbsp* salad oil (not olive)

a few sprigs of basil

---

1 Peel and wash the potatoes then grate coarsely. Wring out in a cloth to remove excess moisture. Add the herbs and spices and mix well. If the potato mixture is too watery, bind with a little flour.
2 Heat the oil in a large frying pan until sizzling. Add tablespoons of potato mixture, press flat with a fork and fry until crisp and golden underneath. Turn over and continue to fry until second side has browned. Garnish with basil and serve hot with cold tongue, salt beef or, in German style, with smooth apple purée, hot or cold.

Photograph opposite (top)

Thyme Omelette

Serves 1
Preparation time: 15 mins
325 kcal/1365 kJ

---

2 eggs, beaten

10 ml/*2 tsp* single cream

5 ml/*1 tsp* chopped fresh thyme

10 ml/*2 tsp* chopped fresh parsley

salt and freshly ground black pepper

25 g/1 *oz*/2 tbsp butter or margarine

1 tomato, sliced

2–3 green or black olives, sliced

---

1 Beat the eggs with the cream and herbs and season with salt and pepper.
2 Heat the butter or margarine in an omelette pan and add the egg mixture. Arrange the tomatoes and olives on the omelette mixture while still soft. Continue to fry until the surface is still damp and the underside set and golden. Fold in half and slide out on to a plate.

Photograph opposite (centre right)

Haddock Parcels

Serves 4
Preparation time: 35 mins
325 kcal/1360 kJ

---

675 g/1 ½ *lb* haddock fillet, skinned

juice of 1 lemon

25 g/1 *oz*/2 tbsp butter or margarine

salt and white pepper

1 onion, finely chopped

45 ml/*3 tbsp* chopped fresh rosemary

45 ml/*3 tbsp* chopped fresh dill

45 ml/*3 tbsp* chopped fresh parsley

---

1 Wash the fish fillets and dry on kitchen paper then sprinkle both sides with lemon juice. Open out large pieces of kitchen foil. Place a knob of butter in the centre of each and arrange the fish on top. Season with salt and pepper.
2 Sprinkle the onion and herbs over the fish. Fold under the ends of the foil to make a fairly tight package. Bake in a preheated oven at 200°C/400°F/gas mark 6 for 25 minutes. Open out on to a serving plate to prevent loss of juices.

Photograph opposite (bottom left)

Desserts, Biscuits and Extras

Even sweet dishes can be enhanced by the addition of the right herbs and there are a surprising number of recipes, like the ones which follow, with unusual flavour combinations.

Peach with Mint Sauce, page 36

Dessert Drink, page 36

Peach with Mint Sauce

Serves 4
Preparation time: 1 hour
3430 kcal/14350 kJ

4 peaches
300 ml/½ pt/1¼ cups whipping cream
4 egg yolks
sugar to taste
150 g/5 oz raspberries
10 ml/2 tsp fresh mint leaves
4 small sprays of mint or a few unchopped leaves

1 Wash the peaches carefully and place in saucepan. Pour boiling water over them, cover and leave to cool. Drain. Remove the skins carefully without damaging the flesh.
2 Slowly bring the cream to the boil. Separately, beat the egg yolks until creamy. Slowly add the cream to the egg yolks, stirring continuously. Rub the custard sauce through a sieve directly into a saucepan. Heat over minimal heat, stirring all the time, until the mixture thickens. Sweeten to taste.
3 Purée the raspberries with the mint leaves and chill. When the custard has cooled, stir in the raspberry mixture a spoon at a time. Add more sugar if necessary.

4 Place the whole peaches into 4 dessert glasses. Decorate with sprigs of mint or a few mint leaves then spoon the raspberry mixture around them.

Photograph page 34

Gourmet Tip
For a seedless sauce, rub the puréed raspberries through a fine mesh sieve.

Dessert Drink

Serves 4
Preparation time: 5 mins
560 kcal/2340 kJ

4 bananas
1 l/1¾ pts/4¼ cups milk
60 ml/4 tbsp cream
15 ml/1 tbsp chopped fresh mint
4 sprigs mint

1 Chop the bananas. Transfer to a blender with the milk, cream and mint and purée until smooth. Pour into drinking glasses and decorate with sprays of mint.

Photograph page 34

Orange Salad

Serves 4
Preparation time: 20 mins
260 kcal/1095 kJ

4 oranges
30 ml/2 tbsp orange liqueur
2.5 ml/½ tsp ground cardamom
sugar to taste
3 sprigs lemon balm, finely chopped

1 Peel and segment the oranges then arrange in a star shape on dessert plates.
2 Mix the orange liqueur with the cardamom and add sugar to taste. Add half the lemon balm leaves. Spoon over the orange segments and sprinkle with the remaining lemon balm.

Photograph opposite

Gourmet Tip
Oranges can best be segmented if the peel, along with the white inner pith, has first been cut away. Then, with a sharp knife, cut out orange segments from either side of the membranes.

Piquant Dessert Snack

Serves 4
Preparation time: 15 mins
850 kcal/3550 kJ

30 g/1¼ oz cream cheese

5 ml/1 tsp mayonnaise, crème fraîche or thick cream

10 ml/2 tsp chopped cashew nuts or walnuts

30 ml/2 tbsp chopped fresh cress, watercress or nasturtium leaves

10 ml/2 tsp chopped fresh parsley

10 ml/2 tsp chopped fresh chives

3–4 slices wholemeal bread

butter or margarine

1 Mix the cheese, the mayonnaise, crème fraîche or cream and nuts with all the herbs, except the chives.
2 Spread the slices of bread with a little butter or margarine then cover each with the herb-cream cheese spread. Sprinkle with chives. Quarter the bread slices diagonally, arrange on a plate and serve.

Photograph (below left)

Apple Compôte with Sage

Serves 3
Preparation time: 30 mins
560 kcal/2340 kJ

---
4 cooking apples
*10 ml/**2 tsp** chopped fresh sage*
*50 g/**2 oz** butter or margarine*
*15 ml/**1 tbsp** brown sugar*
white pepper
---

1 Peel and core the apple, slice thinly and put into a saucepan with a small amount of water, just enough to prevent burning. Cover and cook gently until apples are soft.
2 Beat to a purée then stir in the remaining ingredients.

Photograph (top right)

Gourmet Tip
The apples can be made more piquant by adding a few crushed green peppercorns. Serve the compôte as an accompaniment to roast duck or pork.

Cheese Biscuits

Makes 20 to 30
Preparation time: 35 mins
1705 kcal/7145 kJ

250 g/9 oz wholemeal flour
*10 ml/**2 tsp** baking powder*
*5 ml/**1 tsp** salt*
*10 ml/**2 tsp** chopped fresh herbs (chives, basil, thyme, tarragon, chervil, etc)*
60 g/2½ oz butter or margarine
60 g/2½ oz cheddar cheese, grated
150 ml/¼ pt/⅔ cup buttermilk

1 Tip the flour into a bowl and toss in the baking powder, salt and the herbs. Rub in the butter or margarine then add the cheese.
2 Using a knife or a fork, work in sufficient buttermilk to make a pliable dough.
3 Place the dough on a floured work surface and roll until about 1 cm/½ in thick. Cut out into shapes. Place biscuits on a greased baking tray, brush with a little buttermilk and bake on the middle shelf of a preheated oven at 220°C/425°F/gas mark 7 for 10 to 12 minutes. Serve hot or cold.

Photograph opposite (top)

Herb Bread

Makes 1 loaf
Preparation time: 1 hour plus rising
960 kcal/4020 kJ

300 ml/½ pt/1¼ cups lukewarm water
20 g/¾ oz fresh yeast or 1 packet dried yeast
*5 ml/**1 tsp** brown sugar*
*5 ml/**1 tsp** salt*
500 g/1 lb 2 oz wholemeal flour
*30 ml/**2 tbsp** dried herbs to include chives, parsley, thyme, rosemary*

1 Mix the water and yeast until dissolved. Mix in the sugar and salt. Add about one-third of the flour and stir for 5 to 10 minutes. Cover with a damp cloth and leave to rise in a warm place for at least 30 minutes.
2 Add the herbs to the yeast mixture then mix in the remaining flour a little at a time to form a dough. Turn out on to a floured work surface and knead for about 10 minutes until the dough is smooth, pliable and no longer sticky. If preferred, use a food processor for kneading. Place the dough in a lightly oiled bowl, cover with oiled greaseproof paper or a plate and leave in a warm place to rise for 1 to 1½ hours.
3 Shape the dough into a loaf, place in a greased loaf tin or on a baking tray and leave to stand in a warm place for at least 15 minutes. Bake on the middle shelf of a preheated oven at 220°C/425°F/gas mark 7 for 40 to 45 minutes.

Photograph opposite (bottom)

Tarragon Vinegar

Makes 1 l/1¾ pt/4¼ cups vinegar
Preparation time: 20 mins

---
45 ml/**3 tbsp** tarragon leaves

2–3 cloves
---
grated rind of ½ lemon
---
1 l/1¾ pt/4¼ cups fruit or wine vinegar
---
1 tarragon sprig with leaves
---

1 Put the tarragon leaves into a 1 l/1¾ pt/4¼ cup bottle with a screw top or tight cork, add the cloves and the lemon rind, fill with vinegar and close tightly. Leave for 14 days in a sunny spot, shaking occasionally.
2 Strain into another bottle through a muslin-lined funnel. The bottle should contain a fresh sprig of tarragon. The sprig should be completely covered by the vinegar otherwise it will go mouldy. As you use the vinegar, top up the bottle with more vinegar. As soon as the flavour starts to fade you will have to start again.

Photograph (left)

Variation
Using the same method, herb vinegar can be flavoured with chervil, rosemary, basil or even rose petals.

Herb Oil

Makes 1 l/1³/₄ pt/4¹/₄ cups
Preparation time: 20 mins

---

*60 ml/**4 tbsp** fresh herbs according to taste (leaves only)*

*1 l/1³/₄ **pt**/4¹/₄ cups olive oil*

a few sprigs of fresh herbs

1 Put the herb leaves into a 1 l/1³/₄ pt/4¹/₄ cup bottle or into several smaller bottles and pour in the oil. Close securely and leave for at least 2 weeks in a sunny spot, shaking gently from time to time.
2 Strain through a muslin-lined funnel into clean bottles, in which fresh sprigs of herbs have been placed.

Photograph (right)

> **Gourmet Tip**
> Herb oils are particularly useful for brushing over meat to be grilled or fried, or for salad dressings.

Basil Mustard

Makes about 50 g/2 oz mustard
Preparation time: 30 mins

| 50 g/*2 oz* mustard powder |
| 15 ml/*1 tbsp* white wine |
| 10 ml/*2 tsp* wine vinegar |
| 20 ml/*4 tsp* chopped fresh basil |
| 10 ml/*2 tsp* lemon juice |
| salt and white pepper |

1 Mix the mustard powder in a glass or porcelain bowl with the wine. Bring the vinegar just to the boil and stir in the basil and lemon juice. Leave to cool.
2 Mix sufficient of the basil vinegar with the mustard paste to form a thickish consistency. Season to taste. Put the mustard into a stoppered jar, close tightly and leave for at least a week before using.

Photograph opposite (top)

Variation
Following the above recipe, you can also make mustard with other herbs such as tarragon, rosemary, thyme or crushed fennel seeds.

Herb Butter

Makes about 250 g/9 oz butter
Preparation time: 25 mins

| 250 g/*9 oz*/1 cup unsalted butter, softened |
| juice of $\frac{1}{2}$ lemon |
| 1–2 garlic cloves, crushed |
| 30 ml/*2 tbsp* chopped fresh herbs (parsley, dill, basil, chives, tarragon, marjoram, etc) |
| 3 pinches of sugar |
| salt and white pepper |

1 Put the butter into a bowl and beat in the lemon juice, garlic, herbs and sugar. Season with salt and pepper.

Photograph opposite (centre)

Herb Mayonnaise

Makes about 300 ml/$\frac{1}{2}$ pt/$1\frac{1}{4}$ cups
Preparation time: 20 mins

| 1 egg yolk |
| 300 ml/$^1/_2$ pt/$1^1/_4$ cups herb oil, flavour according to taste |
| a pinch of white pepper |
| 5 ml/*1 tsp* lemon juice |

1 Put the egg yolk into a bowl and beat thoroughly. Add the oil a drop at a time, stirring continuously. Finally stir in the pepper and the lemon juice. Keep the mayonnaise cool and covered in the refrigerator for 1 to 2 weeks.

Photograph opposite (bottom)

> ### Gourmet Tip
> If you prefer, you can also mix chopped fresh or dried herbs into the mayonnaise. Please note that when you do this all ingredients must be at room temperature, otherwise the mayonnaise will become runny. If this should happen, put 10 ml/2 tsp of boiling water into a clean glass bowl and beat in the mayonnaise a drop at a time.

Bouquet Garni

2–3 stalks of parsley
1 bay leaf
1 sprig thyme or rosemary
1 small leek, chopped

1 Tie ingredients up in a piece of muslin to form a sachet.
2 Add to soups, stocks or stews while cooking and remove before serving.

Provence Spices

45 ml/**3 tbsp** dried rosemary
45 ml/**3 tbsp** dried thyme
45 ml/**3 tbsp** dried savoury
30 ml/**2 tbsp** dried orange peel
10 ml/**2 tsp** dried lavender flowers
30 ml/**2 tbsp** dried hyssop (optional)
10 ml/**2 tsp** ground cloves
2 bay leaves
5 ml/**1 tsp** ground nutmeg

1 Grind the ingredients finely with a pestle and mortar or in a food processor and keep in a tightly closed jar.
2 This spice seasoning mixture can be used with all kinds of meat and poultry.

Italian Seasoning

45 ml/**3 tbsp** dried rosemary	
30 ml/**2 tbsp** dried oregano	
5 ml/**1 tsp** dried sage	
10 ml/**2 tsp** white pepper	
15 ml/**1 tbsp** freshly ground black pepper	
30 ml/**2 tbsp** ground cumin	
10 ml/**2 tsp** ground ginger	
15 ml/**1 tbsp** salt	
10 ml/**2 tsp** garlic salt	
5 ml/**1 tsp** garlic powder	

1 Mix the ingredients well together. This seasoning mixture is suitable for soups, sauces and meat dishes.

Minced Meat Seasoning

15 ml/**1 tbsp** dried thyme	
1 bay leaf	
10 ml/**2 tsp** dried oregano	
10 ml/**2 tsp** dried lemon peel	
5 ml/**1 tsp** ground cloves	
10 ml/**2 tsp** black peppercorns	

1 Grind all the ingredients finely with a pestle and mortar or in a food processor and keep in a tightly closed jar.

Index of Recipes

Apple Compôte with Sage	39
Barbecue Sauce	20
Basil Mustard	44
Bouquet Garni	46
Cheese Biscuits	40
Chicken with Tarragon in Cream Sauce	28
Chicken with Tarragon, Honey	27
Chicken Livers with Sage	28
Dessert Drink	36
Fish Pot, Rustic	31
French Sandwich	18
Haddock Parcels	32
Herb Bread	40
Herb Butter	44
Herb Mayonnaise	44
Herb Mushrooms	16
Herb Oil	43
Herb Salad	19
Herb Soup, American	16
Italian Seasoning	47
Lamb Cutlets with Thyme	24
Meat Nuggets, Italian-Style	28
Minced Meat Seasoning	47
Orange Salad	36
Peach with Mint Sauce	36
Pesto Sauce	20
Piquant Dessert Snack	38
Pork, Herb Roast	24
Potato Pancakes, Herb	32
Provence Spices	46
Sorrel Sauce	20
Tarragon Soup	16
Tarragon Vinegar	42
Thyme Omelette	32
Veal Cutlet with Mixed Herbs	24

foulsham
Yeovil Road, Slough, Berkshire, SL1 4JH

ISBN 0-572-01858-4

This English language edition copyright © 1993 W. Foulsham & Co. Ltd
Originally published by Falken-Verlag, GmbH, Niedernhausen TS, Germany
Photographs copyright © Falken Verlag

All rights reserved.
The Copyright Act (1956) prohibits (subject to certain very limited exceptions) the making of copies of any copyright work or of a substantial part of such a work, including the making of copies by photocopying or similar process. Written permission to make a copy or copies must therefore normally be obtained from the publisher in advance. It is advisable also to consult the publisher if in any doubt as to the legality of any copying which is to be undertaken.

Printed in Portugal